THE STATE OF LOVE

A COLLECTION OF MY POEMS

AAQIB JAVAID AZAAN

ISBN 979-888521705-7

"Dedicated to my only inspiration, my family

Mom, Dad, My sisters and Jaany"

Contents

Contents

Contents

Foreword

My English teacher used to tell me that I'm a little creative and good at writing, but I wasn't very interested in studies or writing when I was in adolescence. In 12th grade, I penned my first poem, which was in Urdu. I told my friends and, of course, Jaany about it. Despite the fact that Jaany is uninterested in poetry, she listened and respected what I had to say, which gave me the impetus to create. I began composing Gazals, Nazms, and English after meeting Jaany in the final months of 12th grade. But, until I was in college, writing a poem was merely a way for me to pass the time.

It was during my undergraduate years that I first heard the term "college magazine." Our English professor once inquired about our hobbies and whether we had written anything in English before, such as poetry, a short storey, or an essay. When it came my turn, I declared that while I have written a number of poems in English, I prefer to compose in Urdu. Professor suggested that I attempt writing in English as well. Days passed, and I continued to improve my writing with each passing day. Despite the fact that I wrote almost exclusively about my love, there is definitely a meaning hidden in each poem that the readers must seek out.

Poetry is not a subject for which one would purchase a book. Newspapers, magazines, and textbooks are the only places where people read poetries. As a result, I believe a collection of poems will not reach the majority of those looking for poetry, but I hope you will read my collection. It's all about love, romance, and the beauty of nature. I'm hoping to get a room in your hearts.

Preface

Listening and reading Enlightening poetry gives you the ability to peer into someone else's world and imagine it in your own unique way. The words are written by a poet when they are motivated by magnificent sensations such as love, fury, pain, or infatuation, but the readers can only feel those feelings by reading and understanding the meaning deep inside.

Acknowledgements

I owe a debt of gratitude to my high school teachers and college lecturers for enabling me to write and comprehend this fascinating subject. I owe a gratefulness to everyone who gave me the inspiration to begin learning and writing. I am grateful to my family, without whom this would not have been possible. Their unwavering love and support motivates me immensely.

I'd like to express my deepest gratitude to my parents, and sisters; Andleeb, Moheeb, and Tayuib. I owe my thankfulness to my friends Rehan, Tabish, Aneesh, Prem, Tufail, and Ishtiyaq for always supporting and patiently listening to my garbled thoughts. Then there's Mehak (Jaany), my inspiration, my life's love, for believing in me, supporting me in my darkest hour, and being by my side in every situation. This collection is dedicated to all of my friends and family members.

Prologue

FOR MY MOM

If I could have been
A millionth of your mirth
Every billionth of mine
Would have taken birth
In my heart, soul and spine
But there would have been a dearth
A dearth of your fragrance
A dearth of you in my girth
I trust only you Mom, and
And if I have to endow my soul
You would have been the one
In my life, your love and your role
Never led me to be melancholous
Your presence will always haul
If someone led me somewhere wrong
And if not you, who is going to maul
Pull my hairs, slap me, and hug
Keep in your heart, me and my soul

1. Hey you jealous moon

Hey don't weep
Don't even sleep
U white half-moon
Just go to sleep
Hey don't stare
Go… go upstairs
Right to the stars
Don't look here
Hey don't you know…?
Where to go……!
My baby .. go fast
Don't be slow
Hey you…. moon, listen
Tomorrow afternoon
I m gonna meet
My own little moon
Hey butter, but please don't mind
Please don't look behind
U know, she's only mine
Thanks moon, u make me remind
Hey listen, listen to me
If u ever could, if u ever see
See her smile, isn't in that me

In her very soul, isn't that me

2. A date

Looking from my window pane
The pleasant morning of july
A thought in my thoughts, under the jane
Aaah….! It will be awesome truly
And then its dawn, totally arcane
Nictitating my eyes, I stood up
Whelving you inside, and going insane
Giggling, I put my white hood up
Limerance in each of my vein
State of my mind totally ineffable
Then, met her, parked my bullet, and ran
Nothing in me was stable
Its been 22 days, a long span
Her arms held me tight
And then, long drive in the rain
The zigzag curves , and my world upright
Ran in the rain, with a little pain
Inside that viewpoint hut, frightened
By the billabong, scary rain
Hugged me tight, when it lightened
In a fear , fear of sane
Back to home, after a soothing date
Wet, romantic, with a cold pain

And, pain of rain, pain of fate
Amidst the talks I looked up from the lane
Clouds wrote her name in the sky
Pointing to that I asked her pain
Don't look at me, look up there in the sky
Wow its M written there
Stop I don't wanna miss the stare
Stop aaqib if u dare
If u dare to love and care
Stopped, she got off
Hugged me , kissed my forehead
See I cant say u bye, cant see off
But u have to go for us , a step ahead
Aaqib, This is the moment I hate
Never wanna loose you, and never
I wanna go away with my fate
I loved u , I do, and I will forever

3. My one in a million

My one in a million
My smile my soul
My moon, my stars, my hellion
She is my world, my essence
The time we spent together
I still feel her presence
The moments we shared
Everything, that was, between us
That is damn cute, worth remembrance
The million moments ,trillion smiles
Thousand fights and the daily nuisance
The promises, resolutions, oaths
Desire to die for you, my limerance
Ok, its still ok, my love , tell me
Am I alright, does I make any sense
I know, I have gone mad.... Yes....!
My each sense have crossed my fence
I am not feeling, same, is tere also same
The dreams we dreamt of, in a tense
I know, are no more, neither I am the same
I know, I have lost the limit of tolerance
The time you told me of yourself
I lost my mind, I lost my tolerance

I lost my everything by the time

I lost in your life my importance

August 2018

A minor quarrelsome

4. In my life

In the dawn, in the dusk
In the dark, in the light
The whole day on my mind is you
You peep into my dreams all night
In the fog in the rain
In every site all the time
Like the roses of the spring
Glooming you in the bloom of my site
On the moon on the mars
You look like an angel of the white
And with the company of the stars
You blink at me in the night
In the cold in the fire
Or may in the autumn inspite
Wanna smile with you, angel
Wanna hug you and hold you tight
In the future in my past
I my could would may and might
I just want only you my life
I want you to be the world I write
Inside me deep in my life
In my world of vision and light
I want to keep u caught in my eyes

I want to see only u with my light and my sight....

July 2017

5. Dream mansion

By the riverfront, after the road
Made of dreams a woody mansion
Silence of forest and noise of birds
In the lap of nature with no tension
Moonlight, twinkling stars and the quite night
Noise of waterfalls in three dimension
A small family, mom, dad, sisters u and me…!
Laughing on silly jokes with full attention
Fragrance of flowers embracing feet
Feet of mom and dad after pension
Kids and mom amazed in the lawn
Amazed with the new invention
Dad's hadiths and long stories at night
All of us anxious about the prophet's ascension
In winters flushing snow from roof
Along with dad, with a little dissention
Roses blooming around the extension
Stiff gentions, no mention, the pretention
In the midst of panjal, that's my dream mansion…..

August 2018

6. TOMORROW

Tomorrow if someone comes to you
And comes again, day after day
Talk about me, about my hue
What will u tell him what will you say
Who was I, where I am now
How we met, how we stayed
Will you tell him my name
Will you feel like the same
And, if he made u sad
Say something about me; very bad
Will you then feel the fear
If u have had lost me, will u like to hear
Will you listen to him, in tears
That they lost me, my nears and dears
And when I was wrapped in the white
They waited for you in the light
That whole day and that night
And the next morning they did what was right
They waited for you to attend the call
To see a text which was too small
But you were not there to listen
You just lost me because you didn't missed me at all
Because you didn't had time for me

But you were my life, my one and all

……..

16-11-2018

7. Getting apart

The first day I saw you
Who were you, I didn't knew
But now that I know you
Why are you doing so
I am sorry.........
But I will never let you go
I can't let you go away
No no no no.....!
I am sorry, if the fault was mine
If it was yours then its also fine
I promise you, all my life
I will love you, my angel, my wife
Like I did, like I do, promise.... Wife
Please don't make me so bad
I am , if I am, I will not do what I had
Without you my angel, u know, I am sad
I can't live without you I can't walk
I can"t sleep I can't talk
If you don't talk to me I can't talk.......

8. Tom and jerry

Tom and jerry, me and my merry
Like they fight, like we do
They can't live, like we do
Tom without jerry, as me without you
They feel, like what they feel
If tom is bad, same jerry do
And same is me, when I see
I also do exactly what you do
None can separate them
The prefect two
Made for eachother
So am I, so are we, so are you
If tom fall jerry also will
Their fate is not their, but upto
But their destinies are upto them
So must we, I feel, do you
Come be my jerry I will be your tom
Be mine forever and I will also be true
Feel my tears, feel my smile, feel me
If time's not with us, I know you are with me
And I am always with you…….
I am always with you…….

06-03-2016

9. The miraculous creation of god

Have you ever peeped into the god's creations
Have you ever raised your gaze into the sky
The billion stars playing over there
With the white cool moon the night's only spy
I do feel the essence of almighty god
His presence in every moment that passes by
The realm of green in the fog
The blooming flowers that never feel shy
The noise of silence and the silence of noise
The noise of streams when you take a sigh
Sigh of peace and sigh of the joy
U touch that water and your soul feel high
The feel of nature that I do feel
Feel like me, give a chance, make a try
Close the eyes and listen to the billion voices
Why they weep why they cry.........!
Why they weep why they cry.........!

25-05-2019

10. Cute little moon

Oh moon….. you cute little moon
Can't you see I need you in the afternoon
When sun was on my head
When I was feeling like dead
Where were you, when no one was here
No no no no apologies…..no… I won't spare
Don't look at me like this, don't stare…….!
I will not talk to you…… go upstair
Listen; listen one thing you don't know
The clouds don't glow
But when I need, they come home soon
Listen, you idiot half moon…
Listen you are the love of my life
Don't you know how much I love
I love you more than the stars love me
More then the love can love love
I am beside you whenever you need
You are my life and my world indeed
Don't search me in the streets of clouds
Look deep into your soul indeed
I will be there always… and always for you
So love me, love me like that, love me like you do……

20-03-2019

11. My valentine

Will you be mine
Till my 90 nine
O life will you….
Will you be my life
Not for now
Not for tomorrow
But till the end of my life
O life my ilfe…….
Listen….
Will you be there
When I will not be fine
Listen….
Will you stand by me
When the world will not be mine
Listen my angel……
You are my past
U are with me
Will you be my future
O my shony…..
Till the time of agony
Will you be there for testimony
That you were mine
And I used to be your shony

O life …. My life
On this 6th valentine
I am sorry but I have the same feelings
And so is my question
Will you be mine forever
And ever and ever
Will you be my valentine
Will you be my valentine
Will you please be my valentine…..
14-02-2019 (valentine day)

12. When I m gone

In the morning, the chirping birds
In the evening, the soothing air
In your midnight dreams, my words
Will remind u of me, of me being there
Look around, don't be afraid
I will be no more, but there
Deep inside you, in your shade
In your soul and the air you share
Don't cry when I am gone
Don't fall prey to the tears
Don't be angry on the world
Be calm, be you, don't shear
I will be ok, there, in the dark
In the lap of earth, with no fear
Fear of death fear of life
I will sleep in the white I wear
I know world of yours, world of mine
World of us when we were near
Will just come to an end, but please
Pray for my peace in your prayer
Because I m not lost I m just gone
Gone to the other world, to find a mere
A mere piece of rest, a mere piece of peace

But I promise, I will be with u always, everywhere

June 2016

13. THE MOON

So cute, bright and white
Stars stare, think and blink
They don't sleep all night
Keep en eye at you like a mink
Sky make traps of clouds to trap you
Sun keeps you in his light
All of them try to catch you, grab you
Do you know, for you, how much they fight
You are the love of stars
You stupid ball of light
Sun keeps an eye on you
You are the Sky's divine right

14. A dream in my dream

A dream in my dream
Blood, a colored red stream
In the river of my soul
The drops of my heame
Fear in my eyes
As the hot red steam
Flatterers all around
Looking at my face
Dust all around
And the fearful haze
The dark in the noon
Blood in the pace
Like the fire of the hell
Filled the whole space
No worries, she whispered
Holding my hand
Accompanying you my love
I will walk on the bars of the sand
In your world of dreams
I had always been
Till the end of my soul
I would be very keen
Keen for your love

Keen to be yours
Just hold on for some time
And the world will be ours

Jan 2017

15. Miles apart but together

You slept with me in the silence of love
I kept an eye on the eyes of my dove
You said me to sleep, but sleep faded away
My love, my sanity, my sleep raided the way
You searched the voice, the voice of my breath
I hugged you so tight, like the diamond wreath

You felt my presence in your lap and the bosom
I slept there in your lap like a spring blossom
I kept trying to catch you, like a paid spy
But you were miles away, like a new moon in the lap of sky
In the snowy night, amidst the moonlight
You stole my sleep, you stole my sight
I just wanna say, I always wanna lay
All the life beside you, forever all the way
Come to me my love, come to my life
Come on my angel, come on my beloved wife

19-01-2016

16. Kashway

On the top of the boulder, aside the kashway
Her eyes shining like the stars in the bay
Her breath fragrant like the air of spring
Her hand holding my arm like a string
Her words like the drops of honey
Yes I am talking about my JAANY
Me and my love alone in the midst of the sun
And the fiery curves of flyover over the ban
Sweat on her bosom like the pearls on the beach
Face that of a moon I always wanna preach
Mountains without trees seems to be of mars
My moon with me and me among the stars
I can't forget my October 19 date
I always dreamt of such an awesome fate
I carried her in my arms and make her step down
As she was not able to step towards home, on her own
She came to me and whispered in my ears
I am yours Aaqib, there's nothing to scare

19-oct-2016

17. My home

Amidst the maples
On a hilly dome
Surrounded by apples
Is my home, sweet home
Among the lakes of god
In the hills, lake after lake
Plums, apricots, when they nod
Aah....! the taste of them going blake
No alarms just the soothing air
Azaan and the chirping birds
Don't stop me to come here
Don't let me lose my words
The pines touching skies
The rains, the falling snow
Sight of colors and my eyes
In search of anamnesis as I grow
Behind the mountains when moonrise
Bigger than actually, it is in its size
Like that of perigee, make us surprise
Azaan that's the beauty of my paradise......

03-06-2019

18. The state of love

Every possible way
That leads me to you
Every single day
Every moment I need you
My love, when I mention
I always mention your name
In my dream made mansion
You are always my dame
I need you above all that I need
In my agony you always came
I had you in my worst time indeed
Indeed my finest chapters have your name
I know there is no love like your love
And there is no world unless you are there
My life be my world all above
Be the colors of my breath we share
I don't know the state it flow
I don't know the state of my love
All I know is you and me
All we should know is this love

23-07-2019

19. Miss you my love

A fragrant essence
Of your body and your soul
A lovely presence
On your bosom of your mole
Creating nuisance
As I close my eyes and roll
Crossing your fence
Kissed your mole and I stole
Stole your every sense
That kept your soul sole
I feel the presence
Of old you in my whole
In my moments as little as pence
In my life, your role
Now upon me is the vengeance
But now that you are gone
In every way I feel your absence
I miss you, my love, I am alone
I am not able enough to hold my sense
I miss your voice I miss your tone
I m going weak I am getting tense
Come back my love come home
I will never let you go and hence

I promise you I will never let you down
Come once, come give me your glance
I am found of your love your moan
Don't kill me with this lanced distance
I am crying, come see my groan
Don't kill me with your absence
Don't kill me, my love, with this lance.......

15-08-2019

20. The reason I respire

I still remember her words
Her glowing face and her attire
She is the only reason of being me
That's why I still live I still respire
I still miss the stills when we were together
Her cute voice and her deep aspire
My every moment belongs to her
I cant live without her like a life on hire
It was her that made me what I am
And I believe its her to make my spire
She made me learn to fight for my goals
She showed me the world I must acquire
She saved me from the evil world
She stopped me from the world of satire
She is my angel my queen and my life
She is the only person in world I admire
I loved her, I still do and I will inshallah
I pray for her to be there till the day I retire
Till the day I retire from being alive
Till my last breath till the time I respire.......

21. The midnight dreams

Midnight, midnight dreams and oracles
Asleep in her bosom, her bound shackles
Far from home, no fear, no obstacles
My world of feelings on the pinnacles
The soothing rain and the heat of soul
Air unable to pass in between, the miracles
Light in the darkness of dark
Her fingers crossing mine, like a spark
Laying beside me, me and my shark
The moments most soothing and stark
The amazing defeat in the game
Her winning smile and the lark
These hours of our life
Our love and the way we strife
Her voice was like a soothing fife
Your trance riffed on me, my wife
A favor from you, I want my life
Till the time I am alive, in my life and afterlife.......

11-07-2019

22. June

20 months ago, June
I saw a dream to have my own moon
And each moment I prayed for u
In the wish of having you here very soon
Now that the day have come
I don't have a million dreams
I do see one, two or some
But promise I only dream of you in dreams
Now that you feel the same
You have come in my life as my life
Your life is mine and mine in your name
I give you my name my world, listen wife
Jaany I knew this, but not you
God, insha'Allah had accepted us
The most almighty benevolent and true
He knows and knows better than us
Love, don't think about this world
They don't want, they go ashes
Live your life, live my world
Don't think of them, they do have rashes.................

07-04-2019

23. You don't know

I know you love me, you need me, I know
I know you know it, you know, you don't know
You are my world, I love you, you know it
You love me, I know, but you don't know
I feel what it will be, like….., like after you
You feel the same, I know, but you don't know
You live here, deep inside me, in my life
You are my life, you know, you don't know
Like me, you love me like I do, like I did
My world, you know, you don't know
This side of your, ravaged me into parts
But, each one of them is saying, you don't know
Is this innocence, arrogance or what else
Unaware of this, I know, you don't know
I am effete, please don't rebuff me
Why I am raving, you know, you don't know

23-01-2019

24. October

Fog of the body, heat of the soul
Like a falling star, the mole
Stopped me, exactly there
I kissed, hugged, but I swear
The dew of july, whole
As a trap, a drop, but sole…….!
Drops of dew, due was the end
End of venge, slowly ascend
Fog all around, the hiding hills
Breeze of heaven, beautiful stills
Blue sky-white earth, deadly blend
Never seen such a scene, o friend……!
Seasons, many, but season of love
Calm, cool, lovely, like a wet dove
Shuttering her wings, and then again
Slow rain, fog all around, and wet again
Not all, but some, one or none
Wants like me to see the half sun
Smiling amidst the clouds, glowing
Glowing in its smile, blowing
The rainy clouds away, fog gone
Terrain once again, are switched on…….!

25. Childish

As you came, I am gonna be the same
Childish, arrogant, stupid and insane
I was wrong, what I did, my love
Your love will never get wane
Your dew on lips, and the deep blue eyes
Your shy wet bosom, like a vane
I went to the moon in search of you
I searched the stars, and I lost my mane
Please be the same, please be my angel
When I grow old, when I need a cane
Stand alongside me and make me strong
Till I lose my sense, till I need you sane
I want you still, I want you till
Till the end of our lives, in each one vein
I want you till my very last sight
Till my very last day, till the pain of pain
Don't weep my world, don't feel the same
When everyone will weep, then only you can
Keep your head up to the god, and pray for me
Be the son my mom dad need, be the blood of their vein
Promise me my angel, you will be same as me
Promise me to fill the place, that will once go vain..........

26. THE CITY OF LOVE

The wonder of love, out of seven
I missed to see, but I was a happy me
Rooms many but one o seven
Gave me you, gave me lots of glee
You, beautiful, like an angel of heaven
I was into you and you into me
In the night of the color of raven
That perfectly perfect night, not like pre
The dew, fog, rain and you
It was an absolute dream, it was not true
The time we were us, not me and you
We gonna miss the planes of paper we flew
The dinner, the biryani, and the taste of sue
The sue that we both have been through
I can forget everything of the day but not you
Your lovely bosom and your hue….

18-08-2019

The city of Love

27. What the heck

A mistake becoming a speck
The most important person to me
The only one for whom i reck
She is not feeling like she does
Who am i and is this a heck
I am eyenig a totally new world
New places new people new trek

Its my mistake that i did to you
I am sorry angel i brought u this
I wanted me to get u the roses
But i am sorry angel i bought u this
I tries to teach you the path of love
I am sorry angel that i tought u this
I tried that i will get a new world for you
I am sorry angel that i got u this

I never supposed this will happen to us
I never imagined this will be the fate
I thought i will make u proud
I never thought a moment that u ever hate
I made u feel like u never thought
I have never seen angel your such a state

I never thought I will bring you here
I am sorry angel I brought you this

18-08-2019

28. Remind me dad

Remind me the days when i was a kid, dad
The days when i was not able to stand
Remind me the time when i was a nid, dad
The day for the first time i held your hand

After seeing me the glee that you and mom had
Remind me first day you carried me to school
The complaints of naughty me, ohh.. sir your lad
The stories and the advices you gave me to stay cool

I know some times i made you feel down, dad
But atleast at times i must have been good too
The absolutely wrong desicions of my own, dad
But for your dreams obviously i tried i stood too

Give me a chance dad inshallah i will make you proud
You will hold my hand like in my childhood you did
When you will listen the audience on the road
Then you will definately say, you did, my kid.....

01-09-2019

29. A kiss

I want a kiss to swipe my tears away
I want a kiss to drive my fears away
A kiss that make me strive all the way
A kiss that make me thrive all the way
A kiss that can cure all my scars
A kiss that will light all my stars
A kiss on your hand with ring of gold
A kiss that can make my after world
A kiss that will absolutly give you light
A kiss after which you will never fight
A kiss after i kiss you with whole delight
A kiss which will blow my eyes, my sight
A kiss i always wanted from you
A kiss you wanted from me tooo
A kiss you kissed me for a very few
A kiss when you were obviously true
A want that kiss after we had some sips
I want that kiss which will make me rips
I want a kiss on your bosom, in the kips
I want that kiss from you on my lips
On my lips, in the kips......

30. Choice

A morning in her arms
A day, all the day with her
An evening with her charms
A night, on the hay with her
A home amidst the mapples
Besides the hill covered with pines
Surrounded by roses and apples
Seeing her always when first star shines
A world with her as my world
A life with her as my life
A heart that can always hold
Her heartache and her strife
Choices many but for me
I always chose her for my life
A choice that she will always be
She will be my wife, in my life

31. Idiot: MOON

Hey you idiot moon
You are still here
Its been a long time, u cartoon
U naughty naughty hare
You dont sleep
Why dont you
Why do you keep
Keep eye on the two
You idiot, its been a year
Have you gone somewhere till then
I think, you are in a fear
Fearing of losing someone then
Ok, tell me do you have some
Do you love the stars, as people say
Have you ever loved someone
Stars, sky or your own shade of grey
Then why you keep searching the skies
From west to east and from east to west
You must have lost sleep in your eyes
That is the reason i think you dont rest
Ok, listen you broken lover
Go and sleep and let me sleep too
Dont look at me, dont hover

Or otherwise. I will fall in love with your hue
Go go go go go to sleep
Its very late, let her come to me
Listen, If you are there, she wont seep
And I think u also hate that to see

32. YOU

I am in love with the loving you
All i want is you my love here with me
I am craving my baby doll for craving you
You know I will die my girl if i dont see
So just come and save me, the saving you
Be with me and i will be anything you want
Be my queen, be my guide, the paving you
You had made me, whatever now i flaunt
Come wash my evil side, the laving you
You dont listen to me in your anger
Ok because i can hold the raving you
I will be there for you in any sanger
I will be the slave of, the slaving you

33. AZAAN

Ace in the deck of cards
Verse of the mystic bards
The fragrance of the nards
The very word of the lords
Deep eyes, beautiful face
Like the moon in the haze
When he looks with lowered gaze
Let my heart almost ablaze
All the word that he says
Fall at me like the rays
To me the attention that he pays
I had been searching for days
Each inch of mine oh my lord
Craving for him and his pard
Beats for him, my heart's every cord
For his love, purity, loyality and the sard
My blood getting black and lime
Without him my word are mime
Why do i miss him everytime
Why, without him my poems dont rhyme.....

34. FOR YOU MY LOVE

For you, for me, for us
I killed every wish of mine
I made you happy each day
I wept, but i kept us fine
I wanted us to be together
Together forever, and ever and ever
Do you remember that promise....!
'Listen, i will not leave you, never, ever'
Now that you are not here
You had left my cleft
I can't tolerate this anymore
I can't handle this heft
Dont you miss the days of our love
Long drives, galls and late night calls
The way we fought on pity things
We weren't lovers were the best pals
What if i ask you to come back
Will you do me this last favour
Will you come and hug me once more
Like me will you be my only craver

35. THE SECOND CHANCE

Sometimes, time is not ours
Sometimes, moments are hours
Stand still with your head up
Try once more inspite of saying, fed up
Life isn't as easy as it seems to be
Make it easy as to your own perceptions
Learn to face the storm of your heart
Face the reality of your own conceptions
If it doesn't work, dont wait for 2nd time
If they say life gives everyone a chance
Evolve out of your past, and change
Change for the future, change your stance
Theres a lot differance in a lion and a wolf
Be a wolf in your jungle, that couldnt be taught
Keep your mind enlighten with trust and truth
Be a man of your soul not just a nought

36. NINE

For us, we craved
For days, we prayed
At least we made
At last, we stayed
We wade and paid
The moments we laid
three zero zero nine
The time you were mine
I tried my spine
But you were like a wine
That time after nine
Gave my face your shine
The metro and the mall
That faluda and the stall
U and me in the dining hall
Your call and our gall
I wanna live in your pretty shawl
The way for us it is halaal

37. WORTHY PEOPLE

They ask me, and I ask them, why
They ask me what makes me cry
I never say but I mean, their lie
And then I ask them, why shouldn't I
But I say, like you, I don't lie
I am me, I am never you, am i
And if I am, so high in the sky
Sooner or later I won't be able to fly
I won't be able to fly, so high
Tired, I will fall down and die
Listen, those who talk of that, the only spy
They don't have time to make others rye
They neither look at bosoms, nor they lie
They keep their gaze up, and they fye
The fear of being in someones eye
To them, is Far more than, fear to die

38. Blood red, RENNETS Bloodshed, PELLETS

Blood red rennets
Bloodshed, pellets
People housed
Doors closed
Restrictions imposed
Kids mozed
Pressed gullets
Talking bullets
Sanguivorous mullets
Eating their pullets
The youth and the sire
The lynching and the fire
The unending satire
Of the heavenly attire
Waiting for the dawn
They dont blink and yawn
Now no need to be a pawn
On their roofs and their lawn
They shouted, they stilled
They sacrificed, they killed
They won and the pilled
On the hearts they drilled

They killed for their motherland
They are one when they stand
Like the particles of the sand
They in themselves, are a BRAND

39. HOME SWEET HOME

November, early dawn
Waiting hall and the platforms
Despite of being in my lawn
Away from my majestic charms
Noise, horns, and the smoke
People of different decentS
Rush, mess, and the stroke
Shabby words and the same accents
I miss that polite language
Fragrant words, and the silence
My heaven for u, I always forage
I love in me, your mighty presence
I don't like this outer world
I love my own people, I love you
I m telling you i cant hold
I m coming home, i m coming back to you

40. KIDS WITHOUT MOTHERS

Today early in the dawn
Sighted a deteriorating spawn
Few kids following a vehicle
Like fishes follow some prawn
It was about a group of eight
In search of some left over pate
In the age of seeking sweets
They were following their bitter fate
As the vehicle started moving
All of a sudden they started grooving
Seven of them held the grip and climbed
Youngest fell down and started rueing
The thing to see was her courage
She stood up and started to forage
Without the fear of bieng crushed
Paved through speedy cars with rage
Crossed the road and started running
Courageous, brave, fast and cunning
Again tried to catch the grip, fell down
Twice she fell but her courage, absolutley stunning
Bleeding, stood up and ran after others
That was his family and who else bothers

People come and watch the show like me
No one help these kids without mothers
No one help these kids without mothers.........

41. BROTHER

Till my life nearly ends
They flow in me like blood
They are gonna set my trends
They are gonna be my best friends
People don't care
They never ever bother
They just stare
When I am with my brother
And I won't spare
Not even the tother
If anyone came here
We will beat like a rother
Listen you people out there
He is my brother
He is the one who care
Yes he cares for me
Because he is my brother
From another mother
He's is my brother
Yes he is my brother....

42. The winter

The rays of December's sun
The almighty god's mighty grace
Fog in the morning with little dun
Dew in the evening with pity haze
Rain in plains, snow on the peaks
Colors in the sky, leafless trees
The setting sun and the burning streaks
All sleeping, butterflies, the honeybees
The veiled beauties, the masked faces
Red noses, pink cheeks, and the dry lips
Snow-covered parks, abandoned places
Lit chimneys, kangris, and salted sips
Winter is the season of togetherness
To stay home and to share the space
Shut mouth and the lost consciousness
To pray and feel god's almighty grace

43. Everyone fades

People these days
With multiple shades
Seldom stays
Very often fades
Like the clouds and rays
Rains and shades
Clans of hays
Dreams on blades
No's and nays
Tears and wades
Shadow's soul plays
No makes and mades
Blunt tongues says
Irrelevant like jades
The blood and slays
The innocent cades
Rich enjoys, poor pays
They kills they hades
The word that azaan says
Literally makes him sades
But again what stays
Everything goes, everything fades
In this world of plays

With time everything fades

44. Until I die

I don't want a life with you
I just want you to be with me
Till I am alive Until i die
Until for me my love you sigh
I don't want to tell
With you my beautiful spell
U made me dream
Made me feel so high
You love me I know
O baby please don't lie
Till I am alive until i die
I just want to wake in your arms
A moon a beautiful night with you
So far the stars, and the shining mars
A world of us, just me and you
You make me scream
And don't let me dream
The whole night you sigh
Make me feel so high
You love me I know
Oh baby please oh please don't lie
Till I am alive until I die
Until I die

Until I love, the way I do
Please dont lie, you love me too
Till i am alive, untill i die.....

45. My fate

The lines of my palm
Know nothing about my fate
To me, if they harm
That is not the reason I hate
I use them as my alarm
And they never wake me late
My swag and my charm
Is the only thing I date
Some times cold sometimes warm
Sometimes guilt sometimes pate
And if u think I am calm
Than you are no one to rate
I am the thunder i am the storm
I am storm's calm prior state

46. Trans-people

I don't know why
They hate us like this
I dont understand why
They feel they are the bliss
I dont know why
They think of us with fiss
I dont understand why
Why dont the hear to our hiss
If someone is deviod of eyes
Its not a sin, and they love them
If someone is lacking voice
Its not a sin, and they love them
If some one is unable to listen
Its not a sin, and they love them
And likewise every disability is fine
But if someone lacks genitalia
It is a sin, and they hate us
I dont understand why
Why people dont understand us
This is also a disability, not a sin
We the trans people are not rationals
We qre like other disables, but different
We are disables with a wrong disability.

47. New world dogs

The men of this modern world
Never scolded and never told
That the emotions they hold
Are not at all worth, bieng sold
The eyes are just buttons on their face
To button off the beauty of the race
They must have lost their shitty gaze
The way they look deep into the haze
The words they speak
The way they freak
Their soul merely creak
Morethan the shameless streak
The reasons the girls should feel sate
Are becoming the ones they hate
The girls once were their fathers pate
Becoming the new world dog's cate
The ones we should love and praise
For them, we are becoming a disgrace
If we are not gonna tie our lace
We the men are going to be a filthy race
Merely a filthy race,
Nothing else a shitty race.....

48. NOTHING LASTS FOREVER

Nothing lasts forever
No dream, no realm
Our desires, just steam
No relatives, no relationships
No friends, no friendships
No love, no love story
No glance, no glory
No styles, no smiles
No tears, no fears
No fame, no blame
Who cares, who came
For years they tame
No name, after game
Only who remember our names
Are Our kids and our dames
They scold, they spare
Besides parents, who care
The world so mean, so unfair
They just know to pare
This world stays no where
Nothing lasts forever here....

and

here it ends

....

see you again

....

9 798885 217057

Printed by Libri Plureos GmbH in Hamburg, Germany